Conchas y Café Zine
Vol. VII, Issue 1

Alimento Sagrado

a DSTL arts publication

DSTL Arts presents

Alimento Sagrado

Conchas y Café Zine
Vol. VII, Issue 1

Cover and Book Design: Luis Antonio Pichardo

ISBN: 978-1-946081-57-5

10 9 8 7 6 5 4 3 2 1

www.DSTLArts.org

DSTL
arts

Los Angeles, CA

Table of Contents

Secret Ingredient

Stephanie Paola Salas

Food tastes better when I eat it with people.
I imagine the lone, primitive human
that protected his food from other hungry souls.
Clans and tribes introduced trust and sharing.
Now, families gather around their tables,
feeding each other comfort-lies, surprise-silence.

I eat my work lunch in silence.
Bite of ham on wheat as people
walk on by. Crumbs fall on my lap—no table
for this thirty-minute interval. Humans
can eat without tasting, but it's like sharing
without loving. Do our senses feed our soul?

Teresa made meatloaf for us four hungry souls.
I was only seven, did not yet know silence.
I only knew that there was love in sharing:
her home, her time, her kids were my nephews, my people.
Melting popsicles for dessert. We felt human
and alive. In those summers, hope was on the table.

Meanwhile, my father's nightmare is an empty table.
Wonder bread, pork n' chicken franks; our souls
can wait for Sunday, when they're fed human-God
transubstantiated wine-blood, wafer-flesh, prayer-silence.
Jesus turned five into five-thousand for His people.
My father's Heaven is this limitless sharing.

The kids at my job don't care for sharing.
With different toys, they still share the tables
and the classroom and the people.
At snack time, cheese balls and marshmallows feed their souls.
We don't misinterpret their silence
as anything less than the hungry minds of every human.

When was the first time I felt human?
My friend put Skittles in my yogurt and convinced me that sharing
was caring. Her spoon, my spoon into pink silence
amidst the mess, the noise of cafeteria tables.
We had forgotten our souls
by then; we could barely digest our existence among people.

Is it human nature to turn the tables,
turn sharing into caring for those souls
who live in sensual silence among blank-faced people?

Gossip at The Water Cooler

Michelle Smith

Interesting it is
Secrets fill their ears
Wanting to be free
Where life passes you by,
but full of labor.

Credits

1–"Remembering the Riots", Jaramillo, A.; Poem–"Brick"; page 30

*2–"Snapshots of South Central", Khuu, J.; Poem–"Yard Dogs";
page 118*

*3–"Snapshots of South Central", Chavez, S.; Poem–"Around the
Block"; page 68*

*4–"Snapshots of South Central", Elizondo, J.; Poem–"On a Saturday
in South LA"; page 180*

5–"Remembering the Riots", Smith, M.; Poem–"Profanity"; page 31

Same "O" Same "O"

Lois Jackson King

Let your words my dear paint a picture
No brush painting, which a mind can see; when the eyes can't

Better still, point to me the house, I'm to go to
Please hurry, to make your point as you speak

It was neatly stated, on just what to do
He said clean your room neatly as well

Have you done all of your homework
Dinner is almost done and I'm hungry

He carried the light weight table by himself
It was not yet dark, he didn't need a light

Is it your turn to fix the breakfast
Make sure you turn my eggs over easy

Wake up time, to get ready for school
I have told you time and time again

He limp on the right leg
Too old to use; the stock of celery is limp

Struggles

Lois Jackson King

Struggles to live, is real; come on and stand on your ground

All lives do matter and your life does too

You can't stay covered, by the dirt of others forever and ever

God took us from the dirt; we are above it, our life, is calling, for action

We all have dark places, which cling to our mind

Things which make us focus on our lack of ability

We all have our own individual worth and value

The "Potato," to compare, has many vitamins, such as, B1, B2, B6 and Potassium,

This "Potato," and other different looking potatoes, can help to fight diseases; as we do in the "Lab"

We are individuals, not similar in all our looks and performances

Many have been given misguided (fake news) information

Which can cause discombobulated thoughts; confusing to the links of reasoning

False information hinders a forward-spirited desire and determination

What can stop, the hindrance, to the dream, the dream from a creative being

We too are from dirt, and like the "Potato," we have much to offer. Take Pride in yourself

Potatoes are of many shades of color; all developed, from dirt; a hidden treasure

We come from dirt; yes indeed. But we are not, as some enjoy, their efforts of throwing dirt

Let us wash the dirt from our mind; like washing off the "Potato," and move toward our goal

Focus on more promising adventures; not only for today, but many of the tomorrows,

Oh potato, potato you have eyes and cannot see what's ahead, and neither can we

Do you not know oh "Potato," you keep us in balance; you are, a good source of "Fiber"

Control Cholesterol, antioxidants, and so many other great things, you do so well

Our inner man, the ability, the need to release stuff, emotionally and physical

Supplying vitamins, you help our inner man, and bring strength to the spiritual

We too, can help lower our blood sugar. We and the "Potato" have much in common

Wasting Away

Sanjui

Behind these innocent feet
Are the rumblings
Of the big men.

Power knows no end to this hunger
Brightly choking
Time melting away

I don't perceive
The abundant vegetation
Fruitful harvests

Layers of a generation
Struggling to survive day by day
Everything is darkness
I ask why, oh, why, why, why, why

Credits

1–4: Karen Grasse, "the pipers played" Conchas y Café Zine; Vol VI, Issue 1

5–6 Tina Fallon, "Loss of Focus" Conchas y Café Zine; Vol VI, Issue 1

7: Michelle Smith, "Full Title" Conchas y Café Zine; Vol VI, Issue 1

8–9: Margarita Severiano, "Mother Earth" Conchas y Café Zine; Vol VI, Issue 3

10–11: Felicia Taylor, "Layers of a Generation" Conchas y Café Zine; Vol VI, Issue 3

12: Margarita Severiano, "Eternal Love" Conchas y Café Zine, Vol VI, Issue 3

13: Lois Jackson King, "My Spirit Within" Conchas y Café Zine, Vol VI, Issue 1

Although

Luz Donis

Father and mother earn bread
offered at the altar
for thanks and prayers

The promised land is riddled
with famine and hate

We must breathe
the same air
and eat from
the same soil

I can't tell anyone
that every meal
is a blessing

Credits

Stanza 1–John Khuu, "an immigrant kitchen"
Conchas y Café Zine: "Alphabet Soup", pg.28

Stanza 2–Veronica Alvarado, "Manifesto"
Conchas y Café Zine: "No Bias", pg.18

Stanza 3–Karyn G., "We must teach our children"
Conchas y Café Zine: "No Bias", pg.35

Stanza 4–Abraham Jaramillo, "I can't tell anyone"
Conchas y Café: "Reclaiming the Space", pg.7

Tormented Be, Struggles But Not Defeated

Lois Jackson King

Tormented be, struggles but not defeated
Draw me near my heat cry
With hidden strength, I travel forth
Inside hold no outside to find
Pushing straight with so much anguish
Fight against ruthless of the river

River, please do me no harm
Spirit of great hope, hold me
Oh the shore, I be pleased
On dry sand peace for me
All challenges are now behind me
To welcome warmth from the sun

Sun accenting your glowing beautiful shine
Visualizing memories mine be mine now
Our forbidden love cross the waters
Purposed desire to swim by night
Coming I may take a miracle

Miracle is miracle be, believed hope
Together the future soon to be
No worry to care; wait there
Stretched out arms and awaiting breast
Beautiful sand lay ahead very near
Many past hours without a crumb

Crumb stomach desires; heart desires you
Closer and closer approach is near
Uncertainty lay ahead I must meet
Love will conquer; no time squander
Vision, clear no failure in me
Rope 'n hand, to our balcony

Balcony meets desires of our passion
Heated moments we longed to embrace
Star lighted night, hand held tight
Touching with silence; gleaming bright eyes
The now time which is our
Peace sharing a cup of coffee

Flavors of a Childhood Memory

Abraham Jaramillo

Every once in a while a strong
craving takes over me, cold or hot
Arroz Con Leche flavors of a childhood memory
sweet milk and cinnamon I can still taste
to a child ancient hands could only had made,
and so they did, today a way I remember my Abuelito

A caring man my Abuelito
to my dad a strong
father figure, my dad always tells me, " he made
a good hones men out of me, yes he had a hot
temper, the old man put me to the test
many times, and left me with a proud memory."

Sweet milk, sweet memory
ingredients that somehow my Abuelito
knew how to mix and each taste
with time became strong
the soul every once in a while needs a hot
dessert, something lovingly made

Rice, milk, condensed milk, cinnamon, and raisins made
this dessert if memory
serves me well, is not how hot,
but how much love you put into it—Abuelito
showed me love is strong

and it has a taste

I have to say, I hate the taste
of raisins, so I made
mine with none, cinnamon Strong
we build up, memory on top of memory
sometimes I stop and think my Abuelito had an Abuelito
who might had liked his a little more hot

In summer I enjoy it cold, but in winter I crave it hot
is interesting to me how weather can change the way some
        things taste,
but somehow my Abuelito
and the way he made
Arroz Con Leche into a memory
breaks a precedent so strong

Hot or cold you know you are taking part of something strong
a lesson from a dessert my Abuelito lovingly made
more than a taste, not just a memory.

The First Supper

Gustavo Ramirez

It's another day
today. It's extremely tough.
Another relapse
Thursday. I'll say, "Enough's
enough." Damn. This feeling's
horrible. It's truly for the birds.

How many times will I sing
this song? It's time to change
the words. Counselor is shocked
and a bit upset. She looks at me
dismayed. "What happened this time,
Gus?" On that fateful day. I chose
to drink. I chose to use. A tightrope
on these fences. Now it's time
to man up and face the consequences.

When we write the story
of my life, what will the people say?
They say I'm the one
who counts. I'm sober
here today. Today I sing

a new song. Los pericos fly
above. The canary
in the coal mine. Song
of the mourning doves. Why
do we mourn this new day? The sun

rises in the east. It's not the last—
it's the first supper. So prepare
to make this feast. The dawn
of faith. The Sabbath breaks. The horizon
shines ahead. Put down poison.
Pick up the host. It's time
to break the bread.

All in a Nut Shell

Lois Jackson King

So what if I act different or speak and look different from anyone else; does that make me less valuable? Many of our homes are across the globe. I did not walk or crawl here. So where is my welcome mat?

Oh what a joke; they call me a nut, because I make myself more useful, than some of the others they also call a nut. They put us all in the same category; even though they take the different use of useful greatness for themselves.

Perpetual energy that will not end; being chopped and whipped, as beaten goes. My size may not be big, but the most important is what awaits on the inside.

Reach up to retrieve, but my true self, was a ground start. Looking toward the outer is a border, a divider. An illness can, and may, come about.

As I reflect, into my unmerited beatings (chopping), my inner spirit never lost hope of a better day and time for me. No matter what we may go through, God has a way of revealing to us our better self and a greater purpose for our existence.

I (we) have a worth and a purpose; no matter what it appears to be, on the outside, our inside is what counts; and will repeat reproduction in spirit and through our life's transition.

Emotions

Katherine Vega

Yearning to fulfill and
end up depleting

Taking in empty calories
my voice gets neglected

Choosing to stuff with donuts
instead of satiating my expression

Thinking of the next meal and
forgetting about telling my next story

Living in the unbalance while the balance continues to wait for me

Choosing the hollowness with fries
Instead of fullness with words

The call, a silent scream
for creativity and love
Is so loud and I can not hear
I can not receive the inspiration

STOP
LISTEN

Take a moment
breathe
expel the story,

regurgitate feelings

Take a bite of a delicious apple, and share my unique language

Feel the life flowing in my body and spark the magic of
soul touching

Allow the gift of receiving and let go of blocking the love
with emptiness

I Run Better on Empty, Sometimes

Stephanie Paola Salas

My mother cooks for our family.
Pero se hace
como que nunca es suficiente.

"Esto es lo que hay."
"Yo sé que no les gusta."
"No puedo hacer más."

Y así se la ha llevado
en estos últimos diez años
de nuestra vida

familiar.
What does she do
with all this dissatisfaction?

Quizá la cocina.

Quizá las comidas
que antes se hacían
con tanto amor

se han convertido
en un medio de alivio
emocional.

Y yo,
llevando bocado tras bocado
a mis labios, también
me trago la culpa.

Soy el recipiente
del cumplimiento
de esta obligación.

Cuando era niña,
la comida no me interesaba.
(¡Como batallaba mi madre!)

Llegue a los catorce, craving it all,
pero la comida ya no me caía
tan suave a la pancita.

Words fell from my pen at fourteen,
sazonando con nueva consciencia,
escenas de amor, trágicas

explicitas, románticas.
I would show them
to my friends, my classmates.

"Look, I wrote this."
"This is my favorite part, too."
I didn't care to be shy. Buscaba

la aprobación por donde caería.
Buscaba el "You are enough,"
when I learned to cook for myself.

Lo mein, meatballs, fajitas, cornbread,
flautas, pot roast, huevos rancheros—
something clicked.

Watching me learn, es como si
mi madre se acordó de la creatividad,
el proceso of trial and error.

After college, I began to put words down.
Not the way my mother put her creations down
on the table before us,

but the way I would put down
my first sleeping newborn, gently,
knowing I probably didn't swaddle tight enough,

knowing
they'll likely wake up, cry,
and I'll have to try

all over again.
But these newborn words,
estas palabras me perdonarán,

serán libre de obligación
serán puro amor,
serán mi arte.

Caerán suave
sobre la pagina
in the same way food

won't settle into my stomach.
Y madre, si algún día llegas a leer
estas palabras, ojalá no sean

acompañadas por culpa.

The Pepper

Lois Jackson King

We have talents; some more than others; but do we use them

Sharing what we have is a great thing especially when it helps
them in a way that truly is needed

David played his harp to bring Saul, peace of mind; and music
is like medicine when presented, at the right time
and right place

The benefits are great and well received. Our talent, we work to
improve; but a natural gift just flows with little effort

Can we be compared to the chili pepper; the benefit is like a
life being separated from a well-known existence,
long-growing surrounding; but then

The one, becomes two, three or even four; the pepper, is more.
The purposed; the seed is the inner most strength, as
the spirit of life is to you, to me

The inner satisfaction; richness in value, without money; not a
doctor, but relieve pain; a form of medicine, but not on
the pharmacy shelf

The presence of even just one may heat one up, as in all things,
decent and in order, and when used properly, the stomach
is well-pleased as the consumer from the kitchen

The method goes hand-in-hand, working together makes a great
stand, so using our talent and our different capabilities
makes us a great combined possibility

Separated for greater use, never losing worth, but increasing in
many lives and history-made arenas

No desperdicies la comida

un poema cento

Luz Donis

Por la inexperiencia de mis aun torpes manos
Círculo de la vida que en esta tierra descansa
Debes comer con juicio

Citas

1–Victor Moreno "Mi cocina en tu cocina" publicado en "Alphabet Soup" Conchas y Café Zine, pág. 53

2–Victor Moreno "Travesía" publicado en "Alphabet Soup" Conchas y Café Zine, pág. 67

3–Raul C. Macias "Gula" publicado en "Alphabet Soup" Conchas y Café Zine, pág. 16

Chroni's (purus caseus hymn)

Nikolai Garcia

O chili
      O cheese
            O sausage casing snap

Lord, you brought your peace
to Whittier Blvd. Thank you
for this heaven with a roof. Here
napkins wipe away sin.

This sacred food, this
smothered blessing, that fills
our stomachs with serenity and
our souls with grace.

O chili
      O cheese
            O sausage casing   snap

The Call of Breakfast

Ani MInasian

Tummy yawns loudly, swallowing
jagged air, interrupting Morning
Pages. Bacon slices stretch
out in a cold pan

slowly awakening to
the warmth, greasing the way
for broken eggs, sizzle! Heat
makes everything whole

again. Coffee grounds nestled
inside a tea bag blanket
float on a cool
waterbed. Ding!

The microwave alarm goes off
water bubbles up,
Steeped in a warm bath,
grounds emerge transformed,

bronze and energized, until smooth
vanilla creamer softens coffee's
bitterness. Another ding!
announces the arrival of dark

brown toast, who along with crisped
bacon, greet the sunny
eggs, instant friends on a plate,

they share everything, toast

with egg, egg with
bacon, then
carpooling on a vanilla-coffee
wave together

they head off to heed
Tummy's call.

A Ritual

Sanjui

Buzzz!! Buzzz!
Alarm goes off

I slide unwillingly
Into the day.
I fight the daylight
As I rub my eyes.

Suddenly I inhale
And fill my lungs
With the aroma
Of the morning dew

Coffee beans
Freshly ground
Fill the coffee pot ready
To brew the life-giving substance
To this lifeless human.

The scent fills this abode
And awakens the most reluctant soul
as the nostrils take in in one breath
the warmth and color of the day.

Morning Journey

Lois Jackson King

Slowly rolling from the bed; neatly pulling up the spread
To the window viewing the day; thank you Lord, I do say
And al baño, to do what I must do, apestosa; stinky, stink
Flush; wash up, brush, gargle then spit; easier than you think
Ritual of Meds before a meal; no problem; just take the pill
Crying my dear empty stomach, it needs to be filled
Bring forth the menu of delight, for the tastebuds to be thrilled
Food by any name, is still food to me; this, I will gladly proclaim
Fixing a good flavor meal, yes, yes, yes, this is my aim
Now I go, a la cocina, where I will start, as I do my part
Slicing, dicing, cebolla, y pimientos, lightly simmering in butter
Toss around in the pan, watching to scramble easy; then to the plate
Hot prepared flour tortillas and coffee they do await
Bite, chew, through the gums; look out stomach here it comes
Smacking, smack, smack; taste real good; just like breakfast should
Now finished; putting things back in order
Place it here, place it there; this is just the daily starter

Morning Coffee

Tina Fallon

Last night, I forgot to prepare it,
my morning coffee helps
accept the day. First I fill

the carafe with water
from the sink; I don't need
the filtered water. Then pour

the water into the reservoir. I grab
a filter from the drawer and push it
in, sometimes it is better

if it's slightly damp so that the coffee
grounds stay put, otherwise they could get
into the decanter and that

could get messy but it doesn't
change its purpose. I gather my confidence
and I secretly show the world,

"Who's lazy now?"
I am filled to the top and ready
to follow along and make

changes where need be.

Everyday

Luz Donis

Yesterday's coffee grounds
emptied on the plant

of the day. Get a sense
of the weather, breathe in

the morning dew. Measure
coffee, water, and how tired

I feel. Cool, clean, nifty

percolator takes a while
to warm up. Don't be so

lazy. Take out "La Olla,"
she boils, bringing out more

goodness. The mug
with the mermaid

kinda winks whispering,

"Add a little extra
cream." A spoonful

of shiny brown raw
granules takes extra time

stirring; dissolving.
Who cares ?

It's my time.

Verdura Chicana

Stephanie Paola Salas

Nací en Peru y en Mexico.
No sé ni como llegué
a Nueva Jersey.

Una señora,
Dorca Reilly,
se enamoró de mí.

I'm part of a famous casserole now.

Los gringos mix me
with milk and soy sauce,
cream of mushroom soup
and french onions.

They bake me
for twenty-five minutes
under three-hundred fifty-degree heat.

I live on.

En otros hogares,
me llaman por otro nombre.

Ejote.

Vowels floating
like my earthy flavor

in the mouth.

Bendecido, verdecito,
acompañado por un sofrito
de jitomate y cebolla.

In the pan,
the flesh of my pod softens,
my skin becomes tender,
with a siiiiiiigh
I relax, just enough,
before beaten
yellow egg
joins the group,
soaks up the oil, the flavor.
It rains salt.

I welcome it.

The Story of the 9

Katherine Vega

Chapter 1

The journey of the loving couple brought forward great beauty

Six girls and three boys that were the result of their love

Father held great pride for each of his nine children and filled them
with life

Mother nurtured each of their nine and bequeathed her strength

Each of the nine had their gifts. Child 1, Girl 1 had curious adventure

She knew she would explore the world one day. Child 2, Girl 2
held pure power

She knew she was in charge. Child 3, Girl 3 had compassionate power

She could instantly find harmony. Child 4, Girl 4, received quiet
wisdom that illuminated beauty

His muñequita, Father called her. He passed the secrets of food
and they shared an adventure

Together they fed the rest. Child 5, Boy 1 was filled with curiosity
and Mother's love

This gifted his sensitivity. Child 6, Girl 5 came in with righteous strength

She was born to right the wrongs in the world. Child 7, Boy 2
brought an artistic eye of life

He shared the gift in his paintings and photos. Child 8, Boy 3 was
given deep knowledge of life

His intelligence was beyond words. Child 9, Girl 6, the baby, she
had joyful power

She brought laughter to the family when needed. Together the
family found strength

Father and Girl 4 continued to create in the kitchen, meals created
with beauty

Mole, Tamales, Birria, Arroz, Frijoles, Quesadillas all expressions
of love

distributed to the rest of the family. Parents from Mexico, enduring in the USA was an adventure

Chapter 2

Father being a bracero, created a nomadic lifestyle giving the children daily adventure

A bracero, father of nine, no healthcare, no self care, a fragile heart brought an early end to life

He was young, 42, Girl 4 was 10, and in an instant, gone was her first love

Mother was shocked and scared, as she looked to her 9, discovered her power

Devastated Girl 4 continued in the kitchen making her father's recipes and sharing her beauty

Mole, Tamales, Arroz, Frijoles, Quesadillas and now Potato Salad. Food provided strength

Together the 9 took their gifts and found the value of work. Work gave them strength

Each contributed. Each used their gift. Not a day went by without adventure

Girl 4 kept cooking. Moved from mole to lasagna, from tamales to turkey sharing her beauty

Girl 1 joined the army, Girl 2 learned business, Girl 3 got married as they found life

Of their own. Boy 1 found motorcycles and fast living. Boy 2 found that art was power

Girl 5 knew what the world needed most. The world needed love

Boy 2 and Girl 6 stayed with Mother the longest, for they never knew Father's love

Mother learned to drive, learned to navigate. In her children she drew her strength

The 9 struggled and shared. They worked and grew. Together they found their power

They grew from girls and boys to women and men to discover

their own adventure

Soon they all became Mothers and Fathers and brought in their own life

Girl 4, confused, shared her strongest language with her children. Food, which was her beauty.

Conclusion

This is a story of a family who journeyed together with love. The Immigrant story is already an adventure.

Language, culture and poverty caused them to rely on their strength. They came for a better life.

Father leaving earth early, allowed them to find their power. Girl 4 needed more than the others to survive, she needed to escape into food, cooking, and feeding, for her to shine her beauty.

And The Beet Grows On

Lois Jackson King

Provided by the Heavenly Creator
Made to enhance mankind's life
Enriches hope of much satisfaction
Fill me as I give honor and thanks
Because you are a production from God
Truly able to feed God's hungry children
Useful, in physical growth and strength
Formed within the earth and gives health to the heart
One color for us all; worth each miracle bite
The Juice is as red as, as "The Blood on Calvary"
An eternal taste of greatness to behold
Living up to your glorious reputation of nutrition
No substitute, for your, Red Ruby God given color
"Creator's manufactured vitamin, on the Pharmacist's list
Splendor to enjoy; from soups, salads, and being roasted
And so sublime when you're sweetly glazed when cooked with love

El trigo

Sanjui

Fui pequeño
Sin destino alguno.
Abrió mis posibilidades
La falta del pan
A Los españoles
1542.

Procesado,
Separado
Sin nutrientes
Cambió mi color
Falta de fibra
Pero con un rico sabor

Esperando danzar
Lentamente
Con unas pizquitas de sal,
El polvo de hornear,
Y un manojo de manteca
Mientras burbujea el agua
Sobre el fuego lento

Una, dos, tres
Giro al ser parte
Del deleite que daré
Al final
mientras
Una mano sabia

Me mueve al compas
Del ingrato gorgorear del agua.

Ayyy!! Solo una mano sabia!

Sigo girando
Hasta pegar la mezcla
Con el agua ardiendo
Pues es así como lo hacia la abuela

Giro que giro
Amasa que amasa
Hasta lograr la consistencia
Exacta
y así formar los bollitos
que tomaran otra forma
para el comal.

Y así poco a poco
Me elevo delicadamente
Y desprendo una aroma
Única, Especial
Que viajo a cada rincón
Dejando en el olvido el tiempo.

—Ay, mama!— se exclama!
—Bendita Tortilla de Harina!

—¡La comida de los dioses,
Tiene que ser!

Tribute to Flour

Ani Minasian

Child of the Earth fertilized
by ancient civilizations, Mother of us
all, rich and poor alike
In the field worker's mid-day bertuj
In the anorexic breadsticks
posing on white-cloth tables
from every corner of the world
we cling to you for sustenance

From powdered ash you grow
and expand a hundred times
filling pans and growling stomachs
soaking up juices and holding
up frosting, even breaking off
crumbs for beggar pigeons

Sacred wafer turned holy
flesh, dipped in blessed wine
our first communion with God
our last supper with Christ and
worshipped with as many names
pan and khleb and hotz
in sickness, our toast and crackers
in celebration, our birthday cake and independence
pie as Christmas cookies and Rosca
de Reyes, good enough for Santa
and Baby Jesus

You live in my warmest childhood
memories, fried in my mother's homemade
donuts, wrapped around tel-banir cheese
or smothered with butter and honey
Saturday morning Cocoa Puffs
Friday cafeteria grilled cheese
and further, back
to the old country we go, to dough
kneaded under my grandmother's palms
to lavash cooked in my grandfather's sunken tonir
to golden fields long abandoned
soaked in ancestral blood

You tie me to forefathers I don't remember
They reach out to me
through you from millennia
past, stretching into
the future. In you
we all live forever

I Was in The Mood to Make Lasagna

Tina Fallon

I was in the mood to make lasagna,
But I didn't have any cheese.
And my house was housed up with too much sauce,
Though our hourglass was full of pepper.
I was thankful for the garden of ripe tomatoes
They were unfortunately eaten by the chili!

Hot outside and sweaty but inside it's very, very chilly
I was in the mood to make lasagna
But my hands were full of tomato!
made myself take a selfie of myself and said,"cheese!"
Directions called for salt'n pepa salt'n pepa
And here I am with a giant tub of sauce.

It was a recipe of my great uncle's sauce
Being sensitive I left out the chili
I noticed how the mood of my family members was peppier
I was in the mood to make lasagna
But yesterday I was allergic to cheese
I invited some friends to step on the tomatoes.

I did not however invite TOM Ato
He's rude, self-centered, deals in drugs and so so saucy
I said my favorite show was Dynasty, he commented, "Cheesy!"
That gave me a strange feeling of chills.
I was in the mood to make lasagna

She uses too much salt, he uses too much pepper

I asked him, "Do you like fresh pepper or grinder pepper?"
He knew my favorite food and yet he grew his own tomatoes
I was in the mood to make lasagna.
I told him I didn't feel like drinking and yet he got sauced,
"Ok, fine!" I said. "The wine is not yet chilled."
Yesterday I had my lunch, a sandwich of ham and cheese.

Mozzarella, Camembert, cheddar and Swiss cheese
Provolone, Parmesan, feta, fontina and jalapeño pepper
Muenster, Oaxaca, ghost pepper chili
Brie, Colby, Jack, Jarlsberg, Roquefort and tomato
Havarti, Gorgonzola, Gouda, Gruyere, with nacho sauce
I was in the mood to make lasagna.

I've had so much cheese that my cheeks looked like tomatoes

Salt and pepper, salt and pepper, Coney Island sauce.

Tom Ato put a chili in my goddamn lasagna!

No Leftovers Cento

Abraham Jaramillo

I was born in the richest ghetto
My Mother always said, "Eat your vegetables!"
Sprinkle with dust
(You can always just eat around the burnt part.)
Take them or leave them

Credits

1–Nikolai Garcia, "Hella Trippin'" published in "No Bias": Conchas y Café Zine; Vol. 4, Issue 1–pg. 4

2–Tina Fallon, "My Mom and Dad" published in "Bread & Nails": Conchas y Café Zine; Vol.1, Issue2–pg. 2

3–Mauricio (Soul On Fire) Moreno, "MD" published in "Cult of Personality": Conchas y Café Zine; Vol. 4, Issue 2–pg. 93

4–Karyn G., "Some relationships are like burned popcorn" published in "Chairs On The Dock": Conchas y Café Zine; Vol. 1, Issue3–pg. 50

5–Michelle Smith, "Maxim: Rules for Living" published in "Demi-Gods and Then Some": Conchas y Café Zine; Vol. 5, Issue 1–pg. 69

Chocolate Royale

Lois Jackson King

Dark chocolate rich in fiber; compare to black women's intellect,
is as to being cypher

A woman of color, that's who I am; dark rich chocolate; I call it
"Chocolate Royale"

Many, many earthly years of working; I do toil

A close relationship, soil shaped by God; to a cocoa bean in God's
earthly soil

I did this, so my children's welfare wouldn't be spoiled

A mother of four children, they are now all grown. They now have
grandchildren of their very own

Sweet, Dark Chocolate, yes I am, and won't melt in the hottest sun

No, not even when things got bad, I refused to get wild and run

I worked hard to feed my children and by the grace of God, I got
the job done

Because of my dark complexion, I was denied many good jobs

Some places just didn't like my shade of chocolate; they were like
a mob

I heard blacker the berry, sweeter the juice. Can the Dark Chocolate
shout that from the roof

But I am happy to be able to say, I am truly blessed

My life has been truly worth the challenges; could it have been
a test

The cocoa bean must be fermented to develop flavor; then the rest

Thank God for the victories in them, which has made what you
see in me

The fermenting life struggles of a woman of color have helped
me to be free

As the Dark Chocolate, tasty and healthy; great as a glass of
red wine

The parallel truth compared to a black woman who is not blocked
or confined

There were so many days and nights my eyes were full of tears, I must confess

During the times of social injustice and health issues, things seemed to be a big mess

But I came through by the grace of God; then moving forward with a made up mind

Not wasting any of my God-given time by looking behind

Doing what I needed to do and trying my best

Leaving to Our Lord God all of the rest.

Beets

Lois Jackson King

How important, is color. Can a color be deceiving
But of course, there will always be someone
Can color hold so much power, which will cause a disagree
The disagreement may be determined by experience or textbooks
Color may just be a diversion; and may
Can it develop into a science or mystery
Seeing what history reveals may be a big help,
Who will take the time to visit history
Conformational match, to what life holds
Fact, we all have "Red" blood; valuable to others
The value is not in the color; the inner source
The "Beet" is a red color, both in and outside, will never change
No matter the human color, the normal inside of all is the same
Interacting one with another; for the good of all mankind
As a "Beet," nutrition, strength, to physical, we as well, to the "Spirit"
Eliminate the increase, of these things
Disengaging in those provocative environments and issues

Mi Negrito

Luz Donis

No tengo ojos
por el pinto
ni el rojo
mucho menos
el blanco

Desde tu enredadero
buscas llenar
un vacío dentro
de mi ser

Eres la labor, sudor,
amor del campesino
Llenas las súplicas
al Señor de Esquípulas
y a Ahmakiq

El marchante de la plaza
desde Jalapa, Jutiapa, Chiquimula o el Petén
te liberó del quintal
por 5 quetzales la libra
Llegas a mi casa suelto
arrullado en el canasto
de mamá

Limpio de piedras y gorgojos
lavado, más negro
brillante

Saltas a la olla de barro
a hervir con tus compañeros
cabeza de ajo, cebolla y sal

Reconocido por rico y pobre
el aroma que emanas
crea el hogar

Cruzo un umbral
cambio leche
por legumbre
Bebo caldo negro
cual nutre
vasos rojos

Colado, frito o volteado
te dejas maltratar

Escalofríos me atraviesan
por oir
a un campesino
"Causa "El Niño"
se perdió la cosecha
no habrá para comer
frijol
solo maíz"

In Gratitude

Katherine Vega

Yes! Yes! Yes I say!
There is magic in the
White secretion
It is said all of creation
begins with woman
God gifted her with the ability to bring in life
And give life
Stepping into earth
the first nutrients received:
Milk.

With this potion our bones
Hair
Skin
Nails
Bodies grow
Minds evolve
Life continues
With the love of Mother's Milk

The Milk can come from her body
Or the body of the beautiful cow

As I cry and yearn for comfort
I am fed Milk and all is well

Hot or cold
It is perfect

I have heard
"It does a body good"
I say
"It does a spirit good"

My body is grateful
For not all can receive this
Powerful liquid

For me it is the greatest gift of life

The Miracle of Milk

Ani Minasian

A mother's love
An infant's prayer
Gift of the sacred god Kamdhenu
Omnipresent from nursery to nursing home
Bathing queens with your ivory grace
The color of peace and clouds in the
sky, angels atop a trimmed tree
Serenity lives in your
stillness, and like hope
you flow eternal

Burrito Baby

Tina Fallon

a Heavenly baby of Innocents
He needed some protein for nourishment
Rice gives those special little sparks
of starch
All I wanted was a tortilla wrapped in something
Cheese, oh yes cheese please is a blessing
I did not want meat but refried
Frijoles, smothering in love as it hugs the ingredients together
It's what I hungered for
I feel happy to be alive as I thrive for another bite
And another day of yummy rolled goodness
Salsa, the
magical spice that wakes
up your buds and
seems to say,
"Now he will grow strong, intelligent and spicy!"

Watermelon

Lois Jackson King

Oh Big beautiful and tight
Stripes of a Tiger, but no teeth to bite
Holding, hundreds of secrets just ripe
Roll around if you will; no higher than the ground
Surrounded by dirt, but wonderful to see
How did you get, such a name
Not from a bottle to be poured out
Time for operation; knife please
Oh my, look at this I see; black spots
Rich treasure of reproducing jewels
A hidden vessel of goodness
Let us share equally; just right
A slice all around; sweet juicy "Water melon"
Little black seeds for reproduction
Rich field of goodness to sell and eat

Heavenly Mango

Abraham Jaramillo

Green, smooth skin, free of sin
transcends into the shades
of the golden hour, the power
of the sun transformed
into succulent yellow flesh

One taste brings sweet heaven to
earth, and all that is left
a pit, a seed, new life,
rebirth, evergreen, forever a prayer
of once again
tasting, the divine.

Avocado Mahalo

Michelle Smith

Avocado Mahalo
Hello guacamole
with your chartreuse colored creaminess
Savored in a bit of garlic,
Cracked black pepper,
Tomato red
Yummy as my mouth delights in the
Tortilla chip crunchiness
In love with you I am
I sculpt you with a butter knife
Donde so Margarita con sal y Limon?
What a variety of seed shapes and sizes
y we mi aguacate en Español
Mi ensalada,
Tomato,
Ceballos,
Ajo
En guacamole y Margarita via Mexico
I also enjoy American avocado toast
Is the Haas one the best and the only store bought variety?
You're beautiful and delicious
Green with envy,
And ripen to a black-coated brown
What an alligator pear you are
Smooth tiny bumps and coolness
A super food,
Vitamins B6, C, E, and K
Laden with potassium and low cholesterol ooh

I'll sculpt you with a butter knife
And halve you into a basket shape
So I can grow your seed
I'll eat you in a turkey and cheese sandwich or burger
Or cook with your oil
Decorate my face naturally masked
Versatile and over 10,000 years old
Avocado Mahalo
You're ageless and timeless
Internationally known
Alegre y no adios!

Refreshing

a cento poem

Lois Jackson King

of a four leaf clover
therapeutic gaining
out of boredom licking
and without enjoying it
restore my spiritual energy

Credits

1–"Rules for Living" by Michelle Smith; page 69, "Demi-Gods And Then Some": Conchas y Café Zine

2–"Freedom Writer" by Fabiola Manríquez; page 126, "Demi-Gods And Then Some": Conchas y Café Zine

3–"Notorious" by Luz Donis; page 125, "Demi-Gods And Then Some": Conchas y Café Zine

4–"Just My Opinion" by Magui Severiano, page 123, "Demi-Gods And Then Some": Conchas y Café Zine

5–"Crystal Power" by Patsy Pantoja, page 65, "Demi-Gods And Then Some": Conchas y Café Zine

Representation

Lois Jackson King

As He cherished His creation and gave of Himself

Firm, and always in the ripe season, perfecting sublime

Tender and ready for a divine mission

Useful in many of ways; even on a loving tray

Bring to my busy day, spiritual awareness

Clusters of picturesque purple splendor

Power to relax arterial wall for my life's joy

Join me in a salad and a steak; as I render a prayer

I enjoy you so much; you are as Grace, to one's health

Created to fight high blood pressure, flu, colds, and helps the
immune system

Full of great possibilities and hopeful intentions

Your true worth is intangible and rich in flavor

Our sacred time together gives me joy and great pleasure

Take to heart, the ultimate and final step you represent

Mornings, bring me to where you are; Holy Communion time

You are more than Concord Grape Juice; you represent "The Blood"

Church

Nikolai Garcia

Every Sunday,
near the corner
of Fifth & Main:
the bacon & egg
on wheat.

Hot holy water
first. Light
cream, no sugar.

The egg fries
& the bacon sizzles,
& the tomato bleeds
from its cut. My
stomach mumbles a prayer.

Table becomes altar.
Server becomes priest.
I lift the sandwich;
I receive communion.

Final Sestination

Mauricio "Soul on Fire" Moreno

Our family was in the middle of Thanksgiving dinner
and everyone complimented my mother on the chicken,
but trouble started as I passed the potatoes.
My cousin asked my uncle about the Orange,
knowing he'd be triggered since his state turned Red.
He turned around and called him, "Snowflake!"

And while the front porch slept under the snow, flakes
of dandruff shook onto the turkey dinner
as my uncle wrung my cousin's neck red.
Auntie Gertrude, squacking like a chicken,
forcing herself in-between, staining her sweater orange,
lost her balance and fell face first into the potatoes.

My senile grandpa picked at the face-covered potatoes,
licking them off his finger as if it were a snowflake.
Mother screamed at my uncle to release my cousin or-anger
her further and face the consequences. "You ruined dinner!"
She grabbed the carving knife, menacingly, out of the chicken
and sliced the turkey breast, only to notice the meat was red.

"The turkey's raw, honey. It's not supposed to be red,"
My dad said nervously as he retrieved the potatoes.
But mom shot him a death stare, and his skin turned chicken.
My uncle stormed outside, embracing the real snowflakes,
while cuzzo sat on the couch, trying not to hurl his dinner
"What type of juice do you have?" he asked. "Orange, and orange."

My cousin meekly asked for juice but mother handed him an orange.
"Squeeze it yourself. I'm done." And she stomped out, in a blur
      of red.
I could see my mother yelling at my uncle as I picked at my dinner.
Dad called for takeout as he threw out the potatoes.
Mother kept yelling as her face turned wet from melted snowflakes
All I wanted for Thanksgiving was a plate of chicken.

Instead, I have a family torn by politics, chicken
drumsticks stuck to the carpet, slices of oranges
stained on the linen, a cousin who's a snowflake,
an uncle who's a racist, A house divided Blue and Red,
a dinner without family, meat or potatoes,
a gathering of strangers, an empty dinner.

We ordered orange chicken and snow peas, flaky
egg rolls and red hot Szechuan beef with no potatoes.
I finished my meal knowing it was globalization, not my family,
that kept me warm this Thanksgiving dinner.

The Funeral (a sestina)

Ani Minasian

I

Don't need more surprises to feed
the anger and exhaustion, more leaves
than flowers in the centerpieces, her special cheesecake
took all night to make. This day's already out of hand.
Since the day we first heard she had passed
I'll do anything to keep grief from taking hold.

II

I tell my heart and tongue to "hold"
as we lean on Waze to feed
us directions, while other cars pass
cutting ahead of us, no choice but to leave
desserts on a tray, wobbling in the back, made tearfully by hand,
while we manage the A/C to preserve the cheesecake.

III

Mellow chuckling over the mention of her famous cheesecake
from family and friends while trying to hold
back their tears, tissues dabbing eyes, one hand
over their mouths. Down the center aisle funeral directors feed
the line of mourners as the casket, gilded with the Last Supper, leaves.
We smile and nod at familiar faces in the pews as we pass.

IV

Family members place on the casket as they pass
a lone rose with their tears, plus one mini cheesecake.
One last look before each one leaves,

stumbling across the uneven lawn, younger arms hold

up elders' elbows. Into the open mouths of other family gravestones,
    I feed

flowers from the wreaths plucked by hand.

V

At the luncheon, around the table, hand to hand

platters of consolation we pass

to the mourners who are ready to feed.

Though I'm stopped from eating the cheesecake

by the grief I can no longer hold

inside, I'll fill up on roast beef, rice pilaf and stuffed grape leaves.

VI

Goodbyes float like falling leaves

in the air, relatives embrace hand in hand,

shoulder to shoulder, longer, tighter they hold

each other, the opportunity for one last hug they can't let pass.

In my lap on the ride home, I cradle a mini cheesecake.

It's not the hole in my stomach I'm trying to feed.

When someone leaves on whose love you feed,

there's little but cheesecake to clasp with your hand.

They pass on only what your heart can hold.

Cento #1

Tina Fallon

a bed of wildflowers held her breath for two seconds only
Browner than the pinto beans in your favorite burrito
dressed in soft pink leaves
"I just need a hundred bucks,"
not even for a Tic Tac

Credits

1–Jennifer Elizondo, "Aphenphosmphobia" published in Conchas y Café Zine; Vol. 2 Issue 1: "siniestro," pg. 13

2–Nikolai Garcia, "Hella Trippin'" published in Conchas y Café Zine; Vol. 4 Issue 1: "No Bias," pg. 4

3–Susan Chavez, "Creative Haiku" published in Conchas y Café Zine; Vol. 3, Issue 4: "Cuadros de Costumbres," pg. 39

4–David Fallon, "Pablo" published in Conchas y Café Zine; Vol. 1, Issue 3: "Chairs On The Dock," pg. 36

5–Luz Donis, "Satisfaction" published in Conchas y Café Zine; Vol. 1, Issue 1: "The Flow of Life," pg. 2

Cafecito

Katherine Vega

The aroma fills my senses,
a signal of the beginning

The aroma of the bean ground
finely, fills my veins with life

Memories of my father come in drip by drip
Into the pot

The pour into the cup
lights my heart

I add the joyous white milk
to balance my taste buds

Clink Clink goes my spoon
I blend the two together

sprinkling the specs of earth
of cinnamon on top

I breathe in the sensation of the beautiful day ahead
and bring the sweet nectar of life into my body to prepare for
the day...

groggy steps. stumble up

Veronica Alvarado

groggy steps. stumble up
and out. breath still
stinking. jaws mouth
wide-yawning. lids break
pitch black seals to yesterday's
tomorrow morning. "buenos días
mija, mi hija," greets me. outside
my bedroom door. the sun
ignites all heavens. a windowless
hallway glows. a warm silky
soft hug embrace. a warmer cup
of cafecito nestles into lanky petite
olive hands. there's no baby here.
her baby always and forever y hasta
en el inframundo. a smooth sip
of dark roast coffee. just like her
gathered cinnamon skin. nostril hairs
come alive. alcahuetan taste buds
to a cumbia dance. to get this
party started right. even dead skin is rattled
alive. the darker the bean. the sweeter
the love. she gifts me
breath y vida con café. the luckiest 40 year old
bebe in the world. chiqueada y sin vergüenza.
i nestle my outgrown limbs back
into her shrunken forever safe-warm
frame. the possibilities are suddenly
endless. así

comienza la vida. así
comienzo mi día.

About the Authors
Sobre los autores

Stephanie Paola Salas

Stephanie Paola works as a substitute paraprofessional for special needs classrooms and as a Weekend Supervisor for her local art gallery. She enjoys both her jobs, but enjoys travelling to the Bay, trying new food, and spending time with her loved ones even more. She aspires to become an educator, a mother, and maybe a policymaker. For the present, she seeks to offer healing, understanding, and new perspectives through her writing.

Michelle Smith

Michelle Smith is a poet and artist working toward producing work that emits love and empathy for people of all kinds. She is a welcome addition to our Conchas y Café Zine family of artists.

Lois Jackson King

Mother of 4 with 11 grandkids, 10 great grandkids. Her writings encourage and inspire, while some may have you laughing aloud.

Sanjuanita (Sanjui) Martinez

Sanjui works as a teacher at LAUSD. She has four adult kids, and lives with two of them and her dog Oreo. She enjoys reading and writing.

Luz Donis

Second generation Guatemalan, raised in Boyle Heights. Trained and worked as a nurse for L.A. County and L.A. Unified. Currently immersed in Vipassana meditation and Buddhist studies.

Abraham Jaramillo

Abraham Jaramillo is a multimedia artist; illustrator, graphic designer, and photographer. His love for the arts began back when he created small sketch galleries for his grandmother when he was 8 years old. A longtime volunteer and teaching artist with DSTL Arts, Abraham enjoys and nurtures the pursuit of knowledge both in himself and others.

Gustavo Reyes Ramirez

Gustavo R. Ramirez is a poet-teacher-student-activist. He's excited to share his newly created mission statement: "I am a leader-servant—a worker among workers. My mission is to co-create peace, love, dignity, well-being, and fairness through leading by example and acting now. I will live life to the fullest with a sense of adventure and fun. I am committed to humble, bold, right action with integrity and courage."

Nikolai Garcia

Nikolai Garcia was raised in South Central; lives in Compton; and works in East Hollywood. He is Associate Editor for Dryland. His first chapbook, "Nuclear Shadows of Palm Trees," published DSTL Arts, is out now.

Kathy Vega

Kathy is grateful to explore food and writing for this Concha's y Cafe! A native of California now living in Georgia, she is excited to share her work and explore the world of food! She sends love to all of the DSTL Arts community!

Ani Gohar Minasian

A descendant of Armenian immigrants and survivors of the Armenian genocide, Ani Minasian is an LA-based writer exploring themes related to tolerance, ethnic history and cultural preservation, self-empowerment, and her own struggle for artistic expression. She has written plays, songs, poetry and short prose in Armenian and English, often blending languages to create bilingual works, and is currently working on her first novel.

Tina Fallon

Tina Fallon has contributed to *Conchas y Café* since 2015 and has published, *The Bin... and Other Pieces of Trash* in October of 2020. She has a BA in Theatre from Cal Poly Pomona and several courses in Elementary Education and Child Development. She loves avocados, piñas and tv!

Mauricio Moreno (Soul on Fire)

Mauricio is an artist and writer, originally from the East Coast. He moved to California to fulfill his life mission of being a writer and sharing the stories of others to bring readers closer together and heal the world. He is currently working on a novel under the mentorship of Nicolás Obregón, and is also in the process of publishing his first collection of poetry.

Veronica Alvarado

my young children, makai y maya, would probably say i work too much. or i volunteer too much. or i poet and write too much. this is who i am. there's too much to feel. too much to do.

About the Conchas y Café program

Conchas y Café is a 12-week workshop series for adults, focusing exclusively on creative writing, literacy, and illustration. Participants have the opportunity to work with volunteer writers and artists on developing artwork that will be published and presented in a triannual 'zine and public reading.

For more information, locations, and dates for upcoming Conchas y Café workshops, contact us by email at *info@DSTLArts.org*.

Acerca el programa Conchas y Café

Conchas y Café es un taller de 12 semanas para adultos, especializando en escritura, literatura, y dibujo. Participantes tienen la oportunidad de trabajar con escritores y artistas voluntarios en el desarrollo de obras de arte que serán publicados y presentados en publicaciones trimestrales y lecturas públicas.

Para más información, localidades, y fechas de próximos talleres de Conchas y Café, contáctenos por correo electronico al *info@DSTLArts.org*.

This program is supported in part by:

DSTL
arts

This publication was produced by DSTL Arts.

DSTL Arts is a nonprofit arts mentorship organization that inspires, teaches, and hires emerging artists from underserved communities.

To learn more about DSTL Arts, visit online at:

DSTLArts.org

 @DSTLArts

 /DSTLArts

www.ingramcontent.com/pod-product-compliance
Lightning Source LLC
Chambersburg PA
CBHW051926220626
47052CB00003B/595